the Chocolate Tree

Traci Dibble

This is chocolate.

This is a tree.

This is a chocolate tree.

This is a chocolate seed.

The chocolate seed will be a tree.

It will be a little tree. It will be a big tree.

This is a chocolate flower.

We can see lots of flowers on the chocolate tree.

This is a bug.

The bug will go flower to flower.

This is fruit.

The flower has to have bugs for chocolate fruit to come.

The fruit will get red.

We get the fruit down.

The fruit has seeds in it.
We get the seeds.

The chocolate is in the seeds.

the Life Cycle of a

bug

fruit

tree

flower

Chocolate Seed

seed

sprout

chocolate

How Chocolate

Sort

Crush

Mix

Is Made

Melt

Mold

Can you find the picture that starts with each letter?

c

t

s

I can match the words to the pictures using the first letter sounds.

bug

flower

tree

Power Words

How many can you read?

a	be	big	can	come
down	for	get	go	has
have	in	is	it	little
lots	of	on	see	the
this	to	we	will	